Personal Defense for Women

Respect, Respect, Respect

http://pangeauniversal.com/

Table of Contents

Introduction

Respect is not something that is handed out based on gender; it is something that is owed to every individual regardless of gender. However, much too often, we see the lack of it when it comes to women. Our cultures find so many ways in which they disrespect women while claiming to do it because they respect women. The smallest things have built up and made the world a place that is unsafe and disrespectful of this gender. This is seen in so many different ways when women are owed respect in every way, just the same as any man.

The lives of women are equally important to their male counterparts, and they need to be treated as such and given the same respect that they are due. But we all are aware of the fact that that is not how things are. All over the world, we see women as victims to so much abuse both mentally and physically. The rates of crime against women are higher than most other crime rates. Does this display respect for women? It is so important for society to open their eyes toward the state of things and actively work to change it.

Although we have seen a lot of changes over the years, it is still nowhere near how it should be. Why are equal rights still something that women are fighting for when the world claims to have modernized and made imminent progress? They see prejudice based on their gender in all aspects of life. All this needs to change for the world to see progress and be one where men are treated the same as women. Although many argue that men are primarily different from women and must be treated as such, this hardly applies to what they are owed equally and that is respect.

In this book, you will be reading a lot about women, what roles they have played and how they are still treated by society. One of the main focuses will be on how this discrimination against women can be dealt with. We have laid emphasis on how women can defend themselves without having to depend on or expect someone else to do it for them. Women should not have to be afraid of stepping out of their own homes at any time of the day fearing for their safety. Not only are crimes against women regularly happening out in the streets, but they also happen right inside their own homes quite often as well.

Our society is so patriarchal that men have been brought up feeling superior in every way since childhood. This works in many ways, and the worst is when they take it upon themselves to think that it is okay to use their physical strength to subdue or harm a woman. In fact, more than half the domestic violence cases are not reported due to the very fact that many women are taught that it is okay for them to be treated that way. There is an important need for this attitude to change. Women are strong enough to stand up to anyone who stands against them and to come out of the situation victorious. It is the duty of each person to work towards the safety and empowerment of women in any place, be it at home or out in the world.

One of the most basic steps to creating a safer world for women is for them to train themselves to be mentally and physically stronger than any bully who tries to harm them. Being able to defend yourself will automatically garner fear in anyone who tries to disrespect you as a woman.

Chapter 1: Women's Status in Society and the U.S.

Society's behavior towards women

To get a better understanding of the current condition of women, let us look at how society treats them as well as their legal rights in the country. The rights that are currently given to women have also been won only after women fought years of battles against the norms that worked against them. They have always had to prove themselves and fight to be given equal human rights to those that men have.

One of the most basic thing that needs to change is how men address the women in their lives. They only identify them as part of the role they play in their life either as their mother, wife or daughter. They need to accept the identity of these individuals as women first. The role they play comes secondary. Men should not be allowed to discriminate against women in any manner and think that disrespecting a woman is something that is ever okay. They are raised right from birth in a way that shows them that women are inferior to them in so many ways while they think of themselves as the superior gender.

Some men might argue that they have never disrespected a woman or hit her physically. But they forget how they have placed their own opinions as the final say in so many matters just because they have the inbuilt mechanism of acting superior in the long run. Disrespect is shown in too many ways to count when it comes to women. Physical violence against women is probably the worst manifestation of this attitude men have grown towards women and what we need to work on. This is what you will be reading and learning much more about further in future chapters.

Women's rights in America

Let us take a look at the legal rights of women in America. Things have changed a lot compared to the past, but we still have a long way to go. Looking at the history is one way of seeing just how women have been discriminated against over the years. The fundamental source of the mentality that led to such struggles is so deep rooted that it still manifests itself in this day and age. There seems to be no end to the belief of men always being considered superior to women. And this is what causes every other problem in their lives.

There are still many countries, like those in the Middle East, where women are still not granted the basic legal rights that just about all other country's judicial systems have granted and accepted as women's rights. Even something like driving is considered an illegal act in such places. In the early days, the sole role of women was considered to be a good wife who raised her children and ran the house. Anything outside this stereotype was found to be improper behavior. It took quite some time for changes to start with girls finally being allowed to attend school. Things were still very difficult until the Revolution in the middle of the 18th century. Women became much more active in fighting for what they believed to be their rights and started using different mediums like books, as well, to spread the word. Soon women took a much more active role in matters outside their households though there was still a long way to go when it came to getting legal rights.

Only in the early 1800s did pre-college and college level education start being provided to women in some places. As you can see, the change was slow but sure and that is the direction we still have to move in. One of the major points was the right to vote finally being given to women in 1920 by the 19th Amendment. Although there was much opposition to it, women used it to their benefit. They formed their political parties and fought further for being granted equal rights in the constitution.

The new age women did not just want to live confined to their homes with domestic duties, but wanted to fulfill their aspirations and have successful careers as well. Over time, they have achieved much of what they wanted. The Declaration gives women the right to take part in politics in every manner, starting from voting to running for a post in public office.

Women have equal marriage as well as divorce rights and cannot be subjected to child marriage anymore. They cannot be made to face prejudice based on gender and may pursue any field of education and career. They have equal employment, equal pay as well as the right to paid maternity leave. There are so many different aspects of where women's rights have been asserted and still need to be. It includes any economic rights like the right to own, inherit, designate property, the right to equal work and pay, etc. Regarding civil rights, they have equal citizenship; the right to sue or serve as a witness, serve in the court of law, etc.

Women have the right to keep their name even after marriage and can initiate a divorce as well as ask for child custody. They have complete freedom of speech, religion and even the right to change their nationality. Socially, they have total control over their own selves and the right to access anything that is accessible by males. They have the right to make their own sexual choices, be it inside or outside their marriage. They are legally free to fight against any mistreatment or harm like rape or trafficking.

Despite the laws against abuse of women, we know just how often it still happens. This is why it is more important for women to be aware of their rights and to empower themselves in any way possible to fight against such oppressors. No secondary person has the right to impose their opinions or choices on a woman. She is free to go where she pleases and to choose when.

She also has the choice of how she wishes to dress as well. Subjecting women to criticism based on such things is essentially against the law, and anyone who mistreats a woman is a criminal regardless of whether they claim to be provoked by some manner of "indecent" dress. Women have every right to do as they please.

Chapter 2: Different Bodies but Equal Ability

Men and women are different anatomically as everyone is well aware. Generally, although not always, men have a stronger build than women. However, this does not automatically mean that a man can at any time overpower a woman physically. Women are just as capable of using their bodies physically against a man.

The essential principle is that no woman or, for that matter, man should have to fear being physically harmed by someone just because they are stronger. But since we all know that all too often there is someone out to harm another human being, we need to take steps against it. Firstly let's take a look at exactly how men and women are different anatomically.

Anatomical differences

Based on the gender, people usually instantly decide that the man must be stronger. It is true that men have more brute strength and their upper body is stronger than that of women. However, when you take everything into consideration, you will see that both have equal advantages and disadvantages when it comes to physical attributes. That is why you cannot generalize and assume a man is stronger than a woman.

Men have an advantage because they have more muscle mass and denser, stronger bones as well as ligaments. Women on the other have a better immune system compared to men. In fact, statistics show that women in the US outlive men by three to four years. There may be many things that man can do, but they do not have the inherent capability and strength to give birth to another human being like a woman. Women have greater resistance to colds and many diseases as well. Many points can prove that men are not superior to women at all. However, here we will focus on how women do not have to fear being overcome by a man's physical strength every time.

Although a man has greater upper body strength compared to a smaller female, if the woman knows how to use her body effectively, she can easily counterattack as well. Using the lower body is much easier in this aspect due to the minor difference in strength. We will be explaining much more about exactly how women can fight a man using their physique. Women who work out or work to build their physical strength will have a much better go at this than others. This is why we lay emphasis on maintaining a fit body.

Tips on being healthy and having a stronger body

If you want to fight off someone who comes at you, you need to be fast on your feet and think quickly. That is only possible if you are healthy and fit. You don't need to be a muscle builder or a fitness freak. However, making a few healthy changes in your lifestyle will help your bodywork optimally.

- Try to do some form of exercise for 15-20 minutes every day; it could be anything from a brisk walk to time at the gym.

- Include healthy food in your diet that gives you energy and does not leave you lethargic or weak.

- Eat food that helps your bones and muscles to grow.

- Lifting weights will help build those muscles and make your punches and kicks more efficient.

- Try to practice some self-defensive moves every day. This will make you efficient when you need to carry them out against an assailant.

Being quick witted and some good moves can make up for what you lack in brute strength. This is something most attackers don't expect. They always believe that the woman will be weaker and panic while they get to do as they please. Instead, women need to turn the situation around on them so that they won't be so quick to expect the woman to be easy prey just by seeing a female walk alone on the road the next time.

Chapter 3: A Fight Avoided Is a Fight Won

Knowing what to fight for, whom to fight and when is very important. In the long run, the best option is to avoid a fight at any time. It may vary depending on the situation and sometimes you may not have a choice in the matter. In all other cases, a fight avoided is a fight won. Your fight may be a physical one or a verbal argument. Either can and should be avoided unless you have no choice. In both instances, it is essential to stay calm and keep your wits about you. If someone deliberately tries to provoke you, you will come out as the winner by not falling for it.

If it is a situation where it is a verbal fight, if you argue back just as heatedly, it may turn into a physical fight that you might regret. In fact, this is one of the most frequent instances in cases of domestic violence. It could be anyone, but we often see that men tend to get more physically assertive when a verbal situation gets out of hand.

One person always needs to stay calm and not let the other person take things out of control. If they are shouting their opinions or words at you, you may respond back, but it should not be in a way that just makes it worse. If both people are equally intent on just getting their point across and making the other admit defeat, the situation will not get anywhere. As we said before, you need to know when whom and how to fight. Fight a fight that you are sure to win. Don't fight someone who is not open to listening to reason or any sensible thing that another person says.

Another important thing to keep in mind is not to fight or argue with an intoxicated man. A drunken man is hardly in a condition to listen to someone talk sense and is more likely to get violent if you provoke them. If the person you live with has a tendency to drink and get violent, the right choice is to walk out and not stay in that situation anymore. If you absolutely have to, try to avoid the person while they are in that state or just go along with what they say. In case of it becoming a violent fight, we will be telling you ways in which you can deal with it or defend yourself at any point in time. But it is best to avoid getting into these situations in the first place.

How to avoid a fight

Learn to stay calm and not react to a situation with anger, panic or frustration. Instead of responding in that manner and giving the other person the satisfaction of seeing you riled up, walk away. If you step back from the fight, they have no one to fight. This applies to you as well, if you are angry, walk away and talk to the person when you are calm. This is especially true when you are facing someone with violent tendencies. You can always talk it out later. Ignore anything negative thrown your way no matter how insulted or aggravated you feel. Someone who uses cheap retorts and insults in a fight is always the losing party. Don't take it personally and learn to realize that those are angry meaningless words from a frustrated person. Answering back is just making you the same as them.

Don't escalate the argument by getting angry and hurling insults. In fact, sometimes if the person is irate and you are afraid they might get violent, you might even have to apologize and say that you were wrong. This does not mean that your opinion was actually wrong, but if a few words can help you keep the situation from turning into a physical fight, this is the better option. Keep your eye on the person and try to defuse that situation before it gets out of control. Don't display aggression since you will be provoking them as well. If all else fails, just walk away.

Chapter 4: The Comfort of Home Safety

Any person regardless of gender or age will usually tell you that their safest place is home. Home is where we associate with words like comfort, safety, haven, etc. And that is exactly how it should be. However, we all know that it is not necessarily the case. This is where home safety measures come in. There may be instances where a burglar or any third party tries to enter your home forcefully and try to cause damage. Taking the right measures in securing your home will help you avoid such circumstances in most cases. Keeping your home and family safe should be the priority. We emphasize this in the case of women who live alone since they are likelier targets for such breaches in privacy. Taking a few basic steps regularly and securing the house in a better way will go a long way in actually making your home safe and making you feel at ease as well.

Basic home safety measures

The following are some necessary steps to ensure that your home is a safe place:

- Lock your door securely whether you are at home or out. When you aren't going to be home, make sure you keep all the doors and windows securely locked especially if the windows are not barred. Many people are careless about their back doors and the one in the garage. These prove to be easy access for an intruder looking to enter the house.

- Keep the lights on as much as possible. Burglars will avoid well-lit places. Keeping all the lights off when you go out of town, usually indicate an empty house to them.

- Remember, never to leave a spare key outside. Anyone trying to enter will first check for a key under your doormat.

- Signs like "Beware of dogs" actually help to ward off unwanted visitors. Keeping an actual dog is even better than displaying a fake sign.

- Let a trusted neighbor know when you will be out of town and give them a contact number to let you know if they see something suspicious.

- Invest in a good quality lock for doors. Also, invest in a proper alarm system from a reliable company. This will set off an alarm as soon as an intruder tries to enter your place. Make sure only your family knows the alarm codes. Find a security company with the fastest response rates.

- Don't keep a note on your door to let people see when you are out since this would be a useful sign for burglars. They are also good at keeping a look on the house, and when they hear the phone ring continuously without being answered, they may discern that no one is home. This is why you should lower the volume of the ringer on your phone when you are away.

- Keep your mailbox locked so that others cannot access any mail inside that may contain personal information.

- Having motion sensor lighting in your exterior lawn or area can help a lot at night.

- You should also be wary of sales executives. Try to avoid them as much as possible. Do not open the door to unknown people. Also, don't give out personal information to someone who claims to be from one of your service providers. Call the company and check first if they sent someone.

Chapter 5: How to Survive as a Single Mother?

It can be quite a challenge to survive as a single mother. Other than widows, it is a commonly seen occurrence these days with many women choosing to raise children on their own. Since things can get hard on your own, it is important to be extra careful. Single mothers are also easier targets for many people. It is important to keep yourself and the child as safe as possible.

Home safety measures for single mothers

- Change the locks on any house you move into and invest in a high-quality one. Keep the keys securely with you at all times and do not leave them with any unreliable person. Only a limited number of people should have access to your keys.

- You should also invest in good curtains to keep away any peeping toms. Letting outsiders see into your house is never a good choice.

- You should also stay very alert when you live alone or with a child. If you hear any weird noises or sounds, especially at night, instantly call someone trustworthy nearby. This could be your neighbor or family. Once you are sure that it is nothing you can always hang up otherwise they can reach your house as fast as possible for help.

- Also, invest in a good home security system as any careful family does. It can be beneficial when you know you have a backup as soon as an intruder tries to break into your house. Installing a camera at the gate will also allow you to check who is at the door before answering.

- Keep the landscaping around your house well maintained and done in a way that no intruders can hide behind large bushes or plants. It should all be visible to you clearly.

Digital safety measures for single mothers

- Digital security is an important thing to consider. Since most people are active on social media, it is easy to find out a lot about them through their posts. Single moms should be careful about what they post online and who has access to it.

- Do not post too much personal information on public accounts.

- Don't post pictures or your home to let strangers know where you live. This is especially more so for posting pictures that let people know that you and the child live alone there.

- In case of dating sites be much more private. Do not give out too much information to strangers. Single moms should be more wary of letting strange men into the lives of their children. If you do meet a man from the dating site you have a profile on, do not bring them to your house or even let them know where you live. Choose to meet in public places like a restaurant or park. Invite them home only when you know them a lot better.

- Single mothers also need to be much choosier about dating any unknown men. You need to be completely sure that they would not cause harm to your child in any way. There are a lot of men who target single moms to get to the child. This can be true for any sexual predators as well as child traffickers. This is why children should not be subjected to strange people entering their environment. Avoid posting too many pictures of your child on social media and let it be accessible only to selected people.

Measures to teach the child

- Teach the child all emergency contact numbers. In case of any situation that seems out of the ordinary, the child should be able to contact a trusted person.

- Teach them not to go with any stranger even if they claim to have been sent by you. Do not send any unknown person to pick up the child from anywhere.

- Make sure your child knows how to open and lock the house properly every time. They should be extra careful about not leaving the door open at any time.

- Teach the child a few basic self-defense measures to use in case any person tries to harm them physically. They should be alert and also know when to run away from any situation that may cause them harm.

- Another thing to keep in mind is not to let them wander off alone even on vacation. You need to be extra cautious in choosing where you go and stay since it would be an unfamiliar environment. Choose a good hotel and stick to tourists' spots that are safe and protected.

Being a single mother can be tough. However, you need to know that it gives you the extra responsibility of caring for your child along with yourself. Be as self-sufficient as possible and don't allow yourself to get careless over the smallest of things since it can jeopardize the safety of your child as well as yourself. Keep all the measures we have mentioned in mind, and it should help you avoid most unwanted situations.

Chapter 6: Safety for Women in College

The years at university are usually the best years for any person. This is when you get much more freedom and often stay away from home as well. Get this kind of freedom might be amazing but with no one to answer to and living alone, it can also be a little scary. Women need to be cautious in college as well to stay as safe as possible even while having fun. A lot of women are victims of harassment and assault on college campuses all over. In fact a lot of studies show that women in the college-going age range are more at risk of sexual assault and harassment. Knowing how to avoid such situations or deal with them can help you to a large extent. You should keep yourself as safe as possible and make sure to deal with any such assaulter in the right manner. It is never the victims' fault and the criminal should always be punished. Take as many steps as you can to keep yourself in a safe environment but learn to deal with any situation appropriately if it should arise.

- Don't wander around alone at hours when no one is around. Try to stay in groups most of the time. There is usually safety in numbers. Isolating yourself makes you easier prey for any predator out to harm. Having someone with you will help you avoid the situation or at least allow you to have help instead of being alone.

- Take lessons in self defense so that you can protect yourself incise such situations arise.

- Avoid places where such incidents of assault usually happen. These are dark, isolated areas like parking lots. Such places are easy for predators to hide in and attack any female who wanders there alone. It would also be hard for you to get help in such a place.

- Don't take lifts from someone you don't know. And don't give one to hitchhikers either. Such impulsive moves can often be dangerous.

- Avoid parties where you don't know anyone even if it may be tempting. Go with someone you know and trust. Also know your alcohol limit and do not cross it. You should be able to go home safe and sound. A lot of guys are more than willing to take advantage of girls who are intoxicated. Also don't accept drinks from others at such parties since it may be drugged. You should also leave the party when your friends are leaving and not stay behind alone.

- If you are a sexually active person make sure to use contraception at all times. Be selective about whom you interact with and stay safe at all times. You need to protect yourself from any unwanted pregnancies as well as sexually transmitted diseases. College can easily be one of the most common places to get in either situation. Either abstain or stay as safe as possible.

- Be polite but firm in letting any unwanted suitors know that they are not welcome. Also avoid being in a situation alone with them. If they harass you more than you are comfortable with, let the authorities know.

- If any college professors or staff make unwanted advances, avoid them at all costs and let someone know.

- Download some safety apps that are specifically designed to help young women. There are some that help you call for help just with the press of a button.

- Keep some pepper spray or such defensive equipment with you for emergency use. Taser guns can also be very helpful. If your college allow it make sure to keep one with you at all times.

- Don't give in to peer pressure at any moment. Every girl has an inherent intuition for self-safety. If you feel that it is not something you want to do or somewhere you want to be, being confident and say no. You are answerable to no one but yourself and you will be grateful for it later.

- Make sure you live in a safe place and with people you trust. Living alone should be avoided. Also make sure your doors are always locked and well secured no matter what the living arrangements are. Keep your keys safe and only accessible to a select few.

- You also need to realize that the attackers are often people we know at least to some level. They need not necessarily be strangers. Trust your instincts about people. If you are uncomfortable about something let it be known and enforce your boundaries. Don't let anyone touch your or even talk in a manner that you don't feel comfortable with.

Steps to take in case of an attack

- In case you do fall victim to assault of any sort try to stay as calm as possible and do the needful.

- Firstly, if you feel unsafe in a situation, try your best to get out of there as fast as possible.

- If someone attacks you, use some self-defense mechanisms you learnt and get as far away from them as possible.

- Reach out for help as soon as you can and inform the authorities so that appropriate action can be taken against the assailant. Reach out to family and friends for support.

- Get medical attention and make sure a thorough check up is done soon after the attack. This is very important especially in case of rape. A forensic exam can in fact determine the direction a case filed against the assailant takes.

- Get psychiatric help for trauma even if you feel you don't need it. Such situations will leave you with some sort of impact or other. Getting help from a trained individual will assist you in the long run and also deal with things in the present.

- Don't forget to file an official report against the assailant. No matter how scared you are of the person or how the situation might turn out, it is important that you do this. A lot of women don't file and allow such perpetrators to get away with their crime. It is important to act against such people and make sure they get their due punishment. Only then will others learn not to act that way again. Anyone who harms you or even tries should be subject to legal punishment.

Tools to carry

A few items can help you in case you find yourself in a situation where you feel threatened.

Flashlights

Carrying a small led light or torch can help you anytime you walk around campus or anywhere alone at night.

Cell phones

Make sure to carry your phone with you whenever you step out alone. Call a friend or someone for help if you feel threatened or see someone follow you.

Pepper sprays

These are small and easy to use but just as effective as anything to use right when someone comes at you. There are different kinds available in the market, and you can easily get one for yourself. Spray it in the direction of the assailant's eyes as soon as they come for you. It gives you enough time to retreat while they deal with the burn from the spray.

College should a good experience that you recall fondly in your later years. This is hardly possible for a woman who feels unsafe in the environment and is subjected to harassment or sexual assault. This is why we need to take as many steps as possible to make the college campus a safe place for them and any person there. Colleges should have firm standards and rules for anyone there and should take strict action against anyone who even tries to assault a woman. The women themselves should be empowered and made aware of how to deal with such situations.

Chapter 7: Safety at Work for Women

It is quite disturbing when you realize that women are not safe, no matter where they are. Some of you might argue otherwise, but it remains true. From home to college, to work or anywhere out on the street, they are victims of violence. Subjecting women to such a situation where they could be attacked at any moment anywhere is very stressful for them. Let's take into instance their situation at work. Sexual harassment in the workplace is yet another common occurrence in America.

Studies have shown that the food and hospitality industry has the most of such cases followed by retail, entertainment and ten legal fields. The other shocking study is of how many cases are actually reported, which comes out to less than 40% of the number that occurs. A lot are reported while most are not. The main cause comes down to the fact that women are still not respected and treated equally. They are subjected to leering eyes, lewd remarks and even sexual harassment much too often at the work place. There are different ways to deal with such things. Firstly women need to know exactly what constitutes as sexual harassment and take note of anything that makes them feel unsafe at work. After that is how to deal with such a situation.

What is sexual harassment?

If any person at work discriminates against you or acts sexually in any manner, it constitutes as sexual harassment and is illegal. Making any sexual comments, asking for sexual favors or touching you without consent in any manner is against the law. It could be someone of any gender and is not specific to men or women as either the perpetrator or the victim. No matter who the harasser is, be it the employer, another employee, other staff or even someone not part of the company, they are subject to the laws against it. If at any moment a woman is made uncomfortable at her workplace due to her gender and subjected to verbal or physical harassment, she can file a case against them.

Questions to ask yourself if you aren't sure if it is sexual harassment:

- Did the person's behavior make you feel uncomfortable and was it unwelcome?

- Was there any comment of a sexual nature in any form?

- Was there any physical advance that made you uncomfortable?

- Was it a person who is at a higher post than you and threatened to affect your work?

- Is the person's behavior detrimental to your performance and mental health?

If the answer to most of these is yes, then you should bring it up as sexual harassment.

How to deal with it?

The first step is always to prevent such situations from occurring in the first place. Employers should make sure they take action to make their workplace a safe place for anyone there. They should make it clear that everyone is subject to strict punishment if any such instances of harassment occur. If it does happen, there should be a correct system of how it is dealt with fairly.

- Try to avoid interacting personally or alone with any person in the workplace who makes you feel uncomfortable or has a previously acquired reputation of misbehaving.

- Firstly women need to know that they should not be scared of reporting the person no matter what level he works at. The employers are not legally allowed to retaliate against the person who files a sexual harassment case. So every woman should know that they are free to act against such people at any time.

- Secondly, if a woman feels uncomfortable about the smallest thing, they should voice what they feel. Let the person know that their comments or advances are completely unwelcome. If it is repeated or taken further, ask someone reliable about it and file a complaint. The first level of charge will be at the work level and then at any court of law.

- Tell your supervisor and employer about the incident and file a complaint officially. Let them know about what exactly happened and also what action you want to be taken against the person who harassed you. Also, letting them know about it also helps you in the court of law if they don't help you out.

- Make it public and let others know so that the matter is not hushed down or brushed over. Other employees can also help you as witnesses or for evidence later.

- Talk to supportive friends and family. Support groups will help you listen to others who have undergone such situations and how they have dealt with it.

- Ensure that the company conducts a thorough investigation and takes appropriate measures that are also satisfactory to you. They should also make sure that such behavior is not repeated and you have no subjected to such harassment again. This could mean that the person is fired or even sent to another location. If the situation is not as far gone as such, they should be properly disciplined and not have to work with you further.

- If the company does not take necessary and satisfactory action, file a legal complaint. The harassment is more than a simple touch or comments; there are cases of rape as well. In such situations go ahead and file the legal complaint right then and inform the company as well. The action against such criminals will be at a much higher level.

How to make the workplace safe for women?

Any workplace or company should take steps to make it a safe place for women. There should be measures that prevent any harm as well as measures to act appropriately against someone who misbehaves.

- Creating awareness about what is right and wrong is the first step. Everyone should know precisely what is acceptable and what behavior will not be tolerated. This lets the men know that the company will act strictly against any misconduct while the women know that they can complain in case such instances occur at any period.

- A strict policy against sexual harassment is a must for any workplace. This should be circulated to everyone and followed strictly.

- A committee should be there to deal with such complaints and investigate and take the correct action.

- The company can also go the extra mile and teach women how to defend themselves in case of any sexual harassment whether it is verbal or physical.

Chapter 8: Weapons to Use for Self-Defense

Learning how to defend yourself is imperative for women. You don't have to live in fear of being attacked and instead move around confidently when you know you can quickly deal with anyone who tries to hurt you. There are many forms of self-defense starting from some basic steps, using weapons and training at higher levels as well. Learning any of it is better than being helpless while someone attacks you. Women may be of smaller built than most men, but that does not automatically make them weak. If they learn the right moves and use the right weapons, no man can hurt a hair on their body. This chapter will let you know more about different weapons that can be used for safety. These could be lethal as well as non-lethal weapons. You will also have to check for the rules in some states about carrying certain weapons. For instance, there are states where you may not be allowed to carry a gun if you so wish. Such places are where the nonlethal weapons would be useful for regular use. Weapons of any kind are meant for self-defense. You can use some to buy time to escape while others can be used to seriously harm a predator who intends real assault.

Nonlethal weapons

If you are not too violent by nature and don't like the idea of carrying guns or knives, there are still other options for you.

- Pepper sprays are one of the most convenient weapons to carry. A good spray will cause the person a lot of pain and temporarily blind them as well. That gives you more than enough time to deal with the person in any way you want or just escape.

- Mace is a tear gas type of spray. It will cause the assailant to cough and choke but is not inflammatory like pepper sprays.

- Stun guns are another inexpensive and efficient option. The voltage of a real stun gun will hurt the largest of men and helps you in such situations.

- Tactical flashlights are easy to carry and helpful as well. A bright light is turned on the eyes of the attacker, and it temporarily turns them blind. This gives you enough time to react or run.

- Beanbag guns are an alternative option as well. A good powered device can knock the wind out of any guy. It is very easy to use and quite efficient.

- Stun batons are like sticks that can deliver a heavy load of power on the assailant. The end, as well as the sides of the device, is electrified. That is why the attacker can't grab it off your hands without getting stunned as well. These are a little bigger than other devices but quite helpful.

- When it comes to home safety, we recommend keeping a sturdy baseball bat around. It may sound cliché, but these can be useful if you suddenly hear a sound at night and feel there is an intruder in the house. A sound hit with a baseball bat will knock any man down or out.

- A Taser may seem like a stun gun, but it is not. They have two electrodes, which must touch the skin of the target for the current to flow through. It is much more effective than a stun gun in stopping the target but is harder to use because it cannot penetrate through thick clothing. However, if you practice enough, it can be used effectively to immobilize an assailant regardless of how big he is.

Lethal Weapons

If the place you live in is dangerous or you are afraid for your safety, lethal weapons might be the right option for you. However, these require much more care than the ones we mentioned above and should only be used after proper training.

- Knives are a standard and easy to carry choice. Most people carry a small pocket or Swiss-army knife in their bags or as a keychain. You could also use a larger bladed knife, but these are not convenient to carry or conceal. Small tactical knives can be carried anywhere and used stealthily against attackers. The blades are efficient in hurting the attacker if you know how to use them well.

- Scarves are an unexpected but highly effective weapon. You can carry one at any time, and no assailant will suspect that you can use it fatally against them. Practice how to use them fast, and you can utilize them as garrote or strangle the assailant.

- Tactical pens are easily available these days. They look like pens but can be used to defend against attackers but cutting or punching holes into them.

While using weapons, it is important to be cautious. Like we mentioned above, make sure that it is legal to carry the weapon of your choice in that area. If not, you might get into a situation with the law there. You should also make sure to pull out a weapon only in a state of defense where your safety is jeopardized, and you should be able to prove this in the court of law if the situation arises. Any weapon cannot be used carelessly and requires some degree of training, some more than others. If you are not comfortable and confident using the weapon, it can easily be snatched and used against you. You could also harm an innocent person nearby if you aren't careful.

Chapter 9: Rape- How to Prevent It or Deal with It

Violence is always alarming and especially so when it is against a woman or child. Sexual abuse in its worst form is rape. Forcing a woman to have sexual intercourse in any form without their consent or against their will is considered rape. The very act is often violent and so traumatizing for the woman that they would rather die than deal with the aftermath of how it leaves them feeling. The cases of rape across the country are uncountable, and each has its own horror story.

Many women do not even report against the rapist because for some reason society has imbibed a sense of shame in victims of rape when they should instead sympathize and empower them. A lot of assailants get away with it when they should be subjected to the highest punishment that the court of law can give them. An ideal world would have no rapists, and all women would be safe to go and do as they please. But as we all know, that is not the case. Instead of punishing rapists and fighting against rape culture, some people blame the victims because they dressed a certain way or went to a certain place that is unsuitable.

Rape is in no way and never the victim's fault. It is always the rapist's fault and the fault of a society where women are still not given the respect they are due. Till we reach the utopia that allows women to live freely, they need to be more careful to prevent rape and also learn how to deal with the situation if they do get attacked.

Rape prevention tips

Acting a little cautiously and being careful will help you to a large extent in avoiding a situation where you might get raped.

- Avoid situations that assailants usually use to attack a woman. This includes traveling alone in isolated or dark places and at night when others are not around. Traveling with others and avoiding such places will reduce your risk of being attacked. Don't walk home alone at night no matter how near it is.

- Stay alert and keep an eye out for anyone who looks suspicious or harmful. Stick to well-lit areas and places where there are other people. If you feel someone is approaching you, scream and run for help immediately.

- Communicate your limits clearly to any man you are with and make it known that you are only okay to a certain level. They should respect your choice and not make any unwanted advances sexually.

- Avoid getting too intoxicated at any place and also do not accept drinks from others since they might be drugged. The rape drug is a common way to attack girls at parties especially during college years.

- Trust your instinct and get out of the situation immediately if you feel that someone might try to hurt you.

- Learn self-defense strategies and use them in such cases. Learning how to defend yourself physically will help a woman to a large extent when a man tries to force them self on her. You can also use the various weapons we mentioned to help you escape or hurt the assailant.

- If you have a vehicle, make sure to keep it well maintained. Don't be careless about filling up the gas or keeping the car tuned. You don't want it to stop working in the middle of nowhere with no one around. Keep all your doors well locked when you drive or wait somewhere. Also avoid parking lots alone as much as possible.

- Another thing to bear in mind is what to do if you are a bystander. If you feel a woman is at risk of being raped or assaulted, don't be someone who does nothing. Assess the situation carefully and see if you can help in any way. You don't have to walk into the situation but can intervene by going and walking with her if you see her alone. You could also call for help if you witness more than you can handle yourself. Showing support and caring for a victim is also more than enough.

Steps to take by rape victims

If you were subjected to rape or sexual violence, it is imperative to take steps against the person and report it. It was in no way your fault and the rapist should be punished while you get the utmost care and compensation.

- Go to a safe place as soon as you can.

- Call for help as soon as you can. Call the officials in your area to report and catch the rapist. Contact your family or friends to get help and support you. Let them know about what happened exactly.

- Get medical assessment as soon as possible. There is a high risk for sexually transmitted diseases, pregnancy or any form of physical trauma and it should get treated medically. You should also ask for a proper report that can be used against the rapist in the court of law. This initial report is necessary evidence for the victim. Medical attention is also crucial for you to ensure your well-being.

- Contact a rape service center to get guidance and support. They are more aware of how to deal with such situations.

- Take your time to deal with what happened. Try not to isolate yourself. Don't blame yourself at any cost. It was not your fault. Trust in a friend or family member and talk to them about how you feel. Bottling everything in will make it worse for you. Getting care and support from loved ones will help you deal with the trauma in a better manner.

- Dissociate yourself from anyone who tries to make you feel worse or tries to blame you for what happened. Such people are what is wrong with this society. Instead, let them know clearly that they're wrong and unwelcome. Some people might not even believe you, but you do not need their validation. Another thing that could make things harder for you is if your family does not want you to make it a public issue and wants to hush things down for reputation's sake. That is when you need to stand up for yourself and talk to them properly. Let them know that you would like their support and will nonetheless take action against the rapist. It is unfair for anyone to expect you to let the assailant go free without any punishment.

- You need to understand that there can be harsh after effects after rape. This could be physical as well as psychological. Post-traumatic stress disorder or PTSD is something that most victims have to deal with. Get treatment to alleviate the symptoms and not allow it to consume you.

- Also, try to join support groups or forums and attend meetings. Talking to other women who have undergone the same kind of trauma will help you. They can understand your pain better and also assist you by sharing how they dealt with it.

- Lastly but most importantly, take care of yourself. Do everything that makes you feel better and right. Stay away from anything that has an adverse impact on you. Over time, with the right help, you will get over the trauma and learn to live your life to the fullest. What happened to you does not define you as a person in any way, how you deal with it does.

Chapter 10: Basics of Self-Defense and Firearm Training

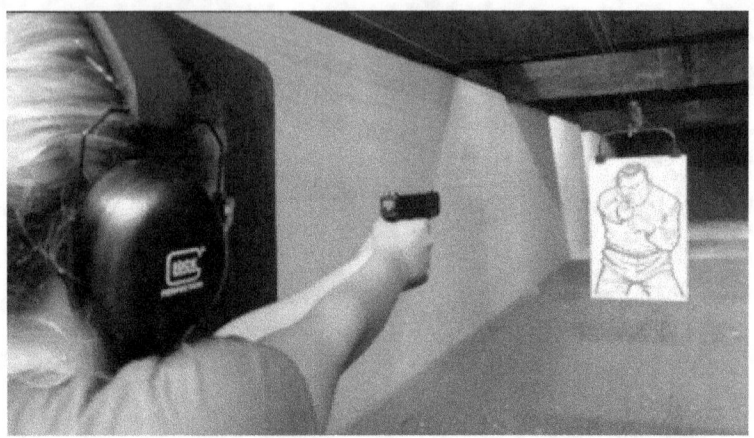

As we have mentioned time and again throughout the book, it is important for every woman to learn how to defend herself. It will play a vital role in getting her safely out of many situations where she might otherwise be harmed. You might be taking all the right steps in staying safe and in cases that are deemed reasonable, but still, end up being attacked. This is why you also need to learn what to do if you do end up being attacked.

We will now be telling you some basic on how to defend yourself when attacked. You will also be getting pointers in basic firearm training. Use these to train yourself and also get some professional help to make you adept at it. This way, you will know exactly how to react when the time comes. The confidence of being good at it will also prevent you from panicking and instead help you keep a cool head as you put the attacker in his place.

Simple defensive moves

The following are some basic steps any woman can practice and carry out effectively regardless of strength and side. If you learn them correctly and get efficient at it, it will be instinctive as soon as someone tries to grab you.

- Learn to throw a straight punch. This is effective when the attacker is right in front of you. Push from your feet and move your hip and fist forward at the same time to get maximum strength into your punch. Aim for the nose or throat, as these are vulnerable areas.

- Throwing a kick to the region if the groin will immobilize any man. Push your hips forward while bending the knee and pushing the heel back. Then extend the leg with force and using the top of the foot, kick the groin area. Kick upward as hard as you can to leave a maximum impact. This is the most vulnerable spot for a man and will buy you time.

- A sidekick is effective when you have some distance. Lift your leg to the level of you knee and then jab sideways at the attacker's knee with force. This will knock him down or at least leave him unbalanced and in pain.

- A knee kick is effective when the attacker is too close to your body. In such a case you can't punch him properly. So try to take a step back or just grab your attacker around the shoulders and drive your bent knee up as hard as possible. Use the tip of the knee to hit his mid region like the stomach or abdomen.

- Learn how to block a punch or slap. When your attacker moves towards you with his hands raised, move your arms out. Keep them a little bent at the elbow and move the forearm inside his arms. Now use your forearm to move his away from you. Use the left hand for this while you prepare your right hand in a fist and punch out at his face or throat.

- If someone grabs you from the back or front around the shoulders, don't panic. Don't try to pry his arms free. Instead, make it instinctive to move downwards and out of his grip. Squirm your way out in a way he does not expect and land a move on him lick a groin kick or some hard punches.

Firearms Training

If you choose to carry a gun and it is legal in your state, you need to get proper training. We will give you a few pointers to let you know what you will be dealing with. Firearms can be very dangerous and may even cause the bearer or innocent bystanders harm. This is why extra caution is required and proper training to use it only as need. You should know the basics about the firearm that you use like its parts, how to load and unload it with ammunition, etc. You should also practice aiming as often as possible so that you don't fire in the wrong direction when the time comes. You also need to be very ethical while possessing a firearm and do not pull it out unless the situation genuinely calls for it. Firing a gun should be your last resort and use it only in self-defense and not fatally.

- Firstly you need to know that there are three basic types of firearms namely rifle, pistols and shotguns. Rifles and shotguns are usually long guns while pistols are handguns. You will usually opt for a gun if you carry it in person and it is also lighter to use for women. Long guns are kept on the property for safety purposes like on ranches or farms.

- The three general parts of the firearm will be the action, barrel, and stock. The stock is the part that holds the action and barrel. The barrel is the part through which the bullet travels. The action is the mechanism used to load, lock and extract the bullet.

- They will have a safety catch which helps to prevent any accidental discharge of bullets from it. This makes it safer to handle. Te safety can be turned off or on.

- Ammunition cartridges are made in different calibers or internal diameters.

- Learn to hold the gun safely and always point it at your target in a safe direction. Aim directly at your target and keep the surroundings in mind. Make sure no innocent bystander will get hurt in case you do have to fire.

- Don't put your fingers on the trigger till you actually have to shoot the gun. If you do, you might actually fire unexpectedly and harm someone.

- You should also keep your gun well maintained like any other device. Clean it regularly and get it checked from time to time by a gunsmith to know it works properly. There are basic cleaning kits for maintain your gun and can be purchased online or at shops.

- Do not ever operate a firearm when intoxicated or under the influence of any drugs. These impair the ability to function properly both mentally as well as physically. Presence of mind and efficient moves are essential for using a gun. Intoxication can cause you to make the wrong choices and also harm others.

- If you own a gun, keep it safely at home. It should not be accessible to any other person and especially not children. Carelessness can cause fatal accidents. Don't ever play around with it or allow anyone else in the house to do the same. Firearms should always be taken seriously even if you feel they are harmless if unloaded.

- You should also be well aware of the local rules or regulations regarding firearms in your area. This is to prevent any unwanted situations that might get you in trouble with the authorities. These are also strict, especially in places where there are more children and are for public safety. You might carry a gun for your safety, but someone else might use it to harm others either knowingly or unknowingly.

How to use a pistol:

- First, you need to know how to hold the pistol or the proper grip. This is what gives the shooter total control while shooting. Hold the weapon firmly and maintain an alignment, which is in natural sight. When you hold the gun with one hand, first form a "v" with your thumb and the forefinger. Place the weapon inside this and use the other three fingers to hold the grip. Let the thumb rest without any pressure and the forefinger on the other side away from the trigger unless you have to shoot.

- Using two hands can give you a steadier grip on the gun. Place the first hand as we instructed above. Then you should place the palm of the other hand over the part of the grip that the other palm does not cover. Place the thumb of the second hand below that of the first. Wrap all the fingers other than the thumb around the fingers of the first hand.

- The correct sight alignment is necessary for firing your shot accurately. When your sight is properly lined, the focus should be on the front sight post.

- Breathing is another important aspect to using firearms effectively. Control over your breath also helps you control your body movements. When you shoot, you should be able to hold your breath the whole time that the shot is fired. This helps to minimize any other movements in the body and makes the shot more controlled.

- Control over the trigger is another factor. The forefinger is placed in such a way that the trigger is between the tip and first joint of the finger. When you squeeze using this finger, the trigger should allow the hammer to fall.

- The stance and position of the body is what allows you to have maximum control while shooting. Depending on the individual's body, there will be a stance that allows them to have the best manner in which to shoot. This varies based on their height, weight, etc. Your position should not only be comfortable but also be one where you can consistently shoot accurately.

- To get more accurate with your shots, go to a nearby shooting range and practice. You can easily find a few which would be easily accessible for you and this is where you can get better basic training for shooting as well. Once you know the basics of how to hold and handle the gun, you just need to keep practicing. An accurate shot is essential in most situations. These ranges will help you become more familiar with your gun and this will allow you to react appropriately when an actual situation arises.

Firearms are not for child play and should be taken very seriously. More often than not, people tend to misuse them to harm others. If it makes you feel safer, then go ahead and get one. But use it only when it is needed and ethically. Even if you use it on an assailant, do not make fatal shots in anger or carelessness, the purpose should be self-defense only. Basic training will help you use the weapon effectively, but ultimately you should know if you are worthy of being trusted with a gun or not. If you have even the slightest doubt then chooses some other weapon.

Chapter 11: How to Survive Any Attack.

You are aware that you might at any time or any day be attacked no matter how careful you are and when you least expect it. However, you are now much better informed about such things than you previously were. We explained a lot in the above chapters but let's now take an overview look at what you should do when you are about to be attacked.

- Firstly, if you are alone and feel someone is about to come at you, move as far away from their range as possible. Also, try to contact someone or call out for help right then.

- Grab at any of the self-defensive weapons that you choose to carry with you and keep yourself alert.

- If the assailant comes near you and no one is nearby then use any defensive strategy of your choice. Spray some pepper spray into their eyes if you have some and run.

- If they have grabbed you or are about to, and you don't have a weapon, use one of the simple moves that we previously mentioned. They are efficient and will buy you time. As soon as you see them writhe in pain, try to run as far as possible.

- Also if you are still not able to get rid of the assailant make sure you don't allow them to take you to another location. They would want to isolate you in a place where they have total control. Try to stay there as long as possible and wait for help.

- If they aim a gun at you, don't panic. Run from them in a haphazard manner and not straight-ahead. This makes sure that they do not to get a direct shot at you. More often than not, the assailant will also be panicking and won't be a good enough shot to aim accurately at you if you run randomly.

- Go as far from them as possible and get help. While being attacked, don't allow yourself to be helpless and actively prevent yourself from being hurt as less as possible.

Presence of mind and proper self-defense methods can help you get out of most situations unscathed. Trust your instincts and be careful no matter where you go or whom you are with.

Chapter 12: The Jungle

It's a jungle out there, and you have to fight for what you want. It is even tougher for women who have to fight through sexism, mistreatment and stereotypes. The important point to remember is that women are natural born leaders who can comfortably lead even during extreme conditions.

In the corporate world, there aren't a lot of women who can climb the corporate ladder that easily. It's statistically proven that women who do work at the top of the corporate ladders tend to make better decisions and have greater leadership effectiveness than their male counterparts.

The reason for this is that women have to work twice as hard as anybody else to get the same results. They face a lot of backlash and problems, which their male counterparts don't face. They have to be at their best at all points of time because they are treated more harshly if they mess up. The point here is that the world isn't simple and you would obviously face a lot of problems when you try to work yourself. You should remember that women are equally capable of being great leaders just like anybody else.

It's easy to dismiss women as weak simply because they don't have the same physical capabilities as men. These stereotypes tend to hurt women who are seen as weak and aren't taken seriously in the business world. This is particularly the case for women who are leaders – they are considered to be too weak to make significant decisions. There are many other stereotypes that further this belief – women are more emotional, their maternal instincts make them more vulnerable, etc. We have to continuously work towards dispelling such myths because these stereotypes can have actual consequences on the way we perceive females.

The best to way dispel such myths is by going back to the basics of our world. Even in the jungle where animals continue to live primeval states, the females are the ones who are the leaders in battle. This is because they are considered to be the ideal leaders – someone who can think things more rationally. The idea is that females have protective instincts, which make them even better leaders as they try to come with ways to protect the herd. This is exactly what makes females better at leadership; they can think more rationally, and they have an instinct that drives them to do better.

This also means that women are capable of taking over and doing better at leadership during stressful situations. The way males' function is primarily based on a show of paper, which can lead to rational thinking taking a back seat. Women, on the other hand, are able to understand difficult situations because they have natural leading skills. Even though many people try to sideline women by stereotyping their behavior, we have to remember that women are natural leaders and are capable of making difficult decisions even under stressful conditions.

The lesson to learn from is that we need to fight these stereotypes to ensure that people don't grow up thinking that women can't survive in severe conditions. It can have an adverse impact on people growing up because they continue to believe that it's the males who are more suitable for leadership. This can discourage people from even trying to work towards leadership positions. This is especially important in a society where we continue to see photos of only male leaders and CEO's. The female representation seems tokenistic and just tries to take away from the stereotypes that women face.

If you're still not sure about women and their leadership skills, then all you have to do is look at how different CEO's deal with feedback. Most male leaders are likely to ignore this feedback because they are so self-assured about their abilities that they don't respond well to criticism. Women, on the other hand, tend to be more understanding and hence, instead of seeing it as an attack they try to rationalize what the other person is saying. This means that they don't let their position rule them but instead listen to criticism when they have to.

Women can be great leaders, and this is proven by how females lead in jungles and how women have always increased leadership efficiency in corporations.

So, we need to explain to young girls who are growing up about how they are natural leaders. This will help in developing their personality in such a way that they continue to nurture their leadership tendencies. These personality traits can be things like nurturing others, motivating others and being more understanding. All of these make a person trust women, more which is why members of a group tend to react more positively to commands or even criticism when women give them.

Conclusion

Awareness of any issue is the first step towards solving problems of this nature. Now that you are much more informed about the issues that women face, you can actively work to improve it. As women, it is very important to stand up for yourselves and not let anyone disrespect you with prejudice towards your gender. We are all well aware of how unsafe it is for women to go anywhere these days and it is necessary to be well versed in self-defense. We have enlisted the many ways in which any woman can turn the situation around to the benefit and fight against anyone who tries to do her harm. Men often underestimate the strength of women, and this will work to their disadvantage when they face a woman who knows how to defend herself. Although the physical differences play a factor, there is no reason to assume that a man can always overpower a woman. It isn't about who is fighting but how. Women need to take the time and effort to make themselves self-sufficient in defending themselves in any situation. While we struggle to get equal rights both legally and in our everyday lives, it is important to learn how to survive in the present world as best as possible. Once women start giving more importance to their physical abilities men will stop trying to use their basic physical strength to dominate over women. Women should be thought of as equal to men in all the ways that matter.

http://pangeauniversal.com/

IF YOU ENJOYED THE BOOK PLEASE LEAVE US A REVIEW WE WOULD REALLY APPRECIATE IT

CLICK HERE